From a Borrowed Land
Shash Trevett

smith|doorstop

the poetry business

Published 2021 by
Smith|Doorstop Books
The Poetry Business
Campo House,
54 Campo Lane,
Sheffield S1 2EG

Copyright © Shash Trevett 2021
All Rights Reserved

ISBN 978-1-912196-64-7
Typeset by The Poetry Business
Printed by Biddles, Sheffield

Smith|Doorstop Books are a member of Inpress:
www.inpressbooks.co.uk

Distributed by NBN International, 1 Deltic Avenue,
Rooksley, Milton Keynes MK13 8LD

The Poetry Business gratefully acknowledges
the support of Arts Council England.

Contents

5	New Words, New Clothes
7	In Your Old Age
8	The Sinhala Only Act, 1956
9	I.P.K.F.
10	Stone Walls
11	Muthumai Kolam
12	புதைகுழிப் பாடல்
14	Grave Song by Cheran
16	The Memorial
17	Things Happen
18	Now that the War is Over
19	Blue Lotus Flowers
	I *What She Says*
	II *What She Says*
	III *What She Says*
	IV *What She Says*
	V *What She Says*
	VI *What She Says*
25	Village
26	I was Na'amah
28	எனது பாடல்கள்
29	My Songs by Vinothini
30	Psalm
32	The Last Mango Tree
33	Gardeners' Question Time, followed by the News
34	My Grandfather's House

For Richard

New Words, New Clothes

I discarded the words first.

And then, for a while, mute silence.
I watched and learnt like a mynah bird.

> அ became A
> ஈ became E
> இ I changed
> to a short, sharp I.

After a while through whispers and croaks
new words emerged
in the borrowed tongue of a borrowed land.

Tentative, tiny and uncomplicated
brand new, pain-free little words.
Their strange scrolls flowed around me.

> *F was once a little Fish*
> *Z was once a piece of Zinc*
> *X was once a great king Xerxes*

For the first time I formed an F, wrote
a Z, sounded an X. In the borrowed tongue
of a borrowed land I dressed myself in them.

I abandoned two millennia
of poetry, mythology and history.
No Pallavan or Cholan could claim sovereignty

over my mouth, my tongue, my mind.
In the borrowed tongue of a borrowed land
in single, stuttering, borrowed syllables
I began to talk again

and the new words began to flow.

In Your Old Age

Appa, do you remember evenings
on the veranda, eating cutlets,
and patties and fried nethali?
The smell of freshly made string hoppers
of hot coconut sambal flecked with
green or red chillies? Do you remember
playing bridge with your friends, drinking
whiskey and arrack? Surrounded
by laughter and companionship
the tinkling of Tamil
of youth majestic with hope and vigour
of the peace of a life abandoned
when the Troubles began?

Now you sit wrapped in a fug of silence
so thick it will not let the light in.
Will not speak of the music of the wind
in the palm trees, or the song
of the skylark by the Murugan temple.
It clots the green of the paddy fields
and the red of the hibiscus
strangles the scent of the open jasmine.
Trophies of a life lost to you
years before your words began to crumble.
Appa, in your muted world
what do you remember now?

The Sinhala Only Act, 1956[1]

Tamil words that lilt, soothing as a lullaby
on a mother's breath. Their *isaioli*   melody
nourishing our *uyir*, a life force   life
marked on a stave imagined
a millennia ago. In whispers
of promises they show themselves
as *paadal* and *kathai* and *kavithai*.   songs; stories; poetry
Our generations were formed
by their fluid *naatiyam*, our voices   dance
tuned to their scripted *sangheetham*.   hymns
And when we dreamed, our dreams erupted
in அs and இs and உs: building blocks   Aa; Ee; Uu
of a nation now without a homeland,
a people now without a place.

And when in '56 they tried to silence
your *innisai*, gag your *uyiroli*   sweet melody; vowels
and eradicate your *meiyelluthal*   consonants
we took to the streets carrying
your *unmai* as our arms. Warriors   truth
of the *Tolkaapiyam*[2] on Galle Face Green
paying with our blood for your right to be.
Oru naadillaathe aatkal, in exile,   A people without a country
bearing the music of your beauty, still.

---

1 The Sinhala Only Act (1956) demoted Tamil from being one of the national languages of Sri Lanka. The Act was met with protests on Galle Face Green in the heart of Colombo. The law was repealed a few years later.

2 This is the earliest written Tamil grammar, believed to have originated, in written form from oral sources, sometime between 10BC and 5BC. This text is a fundamental cornerstone of Tamil Literature.

I.P.K.F.

The Indian Peace Keeping Force.
Protectors of the powerless
defenders of the disenfranchised.

We threw garlands around their semi-automatics
strew petals beneath their T-72s
and welcomed them with prasadam.

To a war-weary population
they were heroes –
our friends, the Indians.

Not for long.

When our garlands broke
and turned to a reddened slurry
beneath marching boots

we re-labelled them
the Innocent People Killing Force.

Stone Walls

I remember the day the tanks rolled up
and we hid in that narrow room at the back
of the house. The birds fell silent.
In a moment of stillness we heard quite clearly
ek, do, teen, fire. Over and over, each shout
followed by a thud, each thud followed
by a crash, each crash and splintering
of our world amplified in that narrow space.

Glass shattered, timber collapsed. Dust
and frass danced in the air as the ceilings
blushed hot. I remember, over the boom
of the tanks, the thin tinkling of the piano
as bullets ricocheted off walls and door
frames. Our hearts paused. You and I
cowered on that floor, petrified.

It took an hour for the house to capitulate
in flames, so the neighbours said later
when they found us hardened into a stone
stillness. Although we returned many times
through the years to that room – on that day,
in that year, when the tanks had done
their job and moved away, we emerged
two bodies deadened to feelings
so cold, so numb, so walled in

that was our tragedy.

Muthumai Kolam[3]

Feet planted in perfect balance
she bends each morning deftly
dotting the floor. Each pulli a prayer
each sikku a curving embrace.

The fish, birds and flowers, her suns
moons and stars, her patterned privations
flow through from the outside in,
a propitiation—

so that he might not disappear
into the darkness, so that her lips
might call him forth from the unknown.
Each curve and syllable of his name
a proclamation of his absence.

For months she has performed
these muthumai kolams for him.

While somewhere
he washes her feet daily
with his tears.

---

3 Muthumai Kolam in Tamil means 'patterns of old age'. Kolams are the patterns drawn by Tamil women in front of houses as an offering to deities. They are made up of dots (pulli) and strokes (sikku). This poem is about the Tamil 'disappeared' in Sri Lanka.

புதைகுழிப் பாடல்
சேரன்

அவன் தனியே
அவர்களோ மூவர்
முகம் தெரியா இருள்
அவர்களுடைய மனதைப் போல

தன்னுடைய புதைகுழியைத்
தானே வெட்டும் அவலம்
நேர்ந்தபோது
அவன் என்ன உணர்ந்திருப்பான்
என்பது
வார்த்தைக்குள் அகப்படாத
குரூரம்.

அந்தப் புதைகுழியின் மேல்
காற்றில்
உறைந்து போயிருக்கின்றன
அவன் இறுதியாகச்
சொன்ன வார்த்தைகள்

காற்று அவற்றைக்
கொண்டு செல்லாது
மழையும் சூரியனும்
கிட்டவும் நெருங்கா

அவன் சொல்லாத வார்த்தைகளோ
மண்ணுட் போய்
மண்ணிலிருந்து மரத்துட் போய்
அங்கிருந்து கிளைக்கு
கிளையில் இருந்து இலைக்கு
இலையிலிருந்து காற்றில்

இடையறாமல்
அலையலையாக எழுந்துகொண்டிருக்கிறது.

அந்தப் புதைகுழியின் மேல்
பிசாசு இல்லை
தெய்வமும் இல்லை
நினைவுச் சின்னம் எனவும் ஒன்றில்லை

ஆளரவமற்ற இரவுத் தெருவின்
ஒற்றை விளக்குப் போல
உதிரியாய் ஒரு பட்டிப் பூ
அதன் மீது
காலம் தன்னுடைய கொடூர
நகங்களைப் பதித்துள்ளது.

அவனுடை இறுதி வார்த்தைகளில்
இருந்தது
நமது தேசத்தின் உயிர்.

Grave Song

    by Cheran

Alone with the three
whose faces and hearts
were hidden in darkness

he dug his own grave.
His distress, the horrors he felt
were trapped within his unspoken words

which congealed in the air
above that grave.

The wind would not permit
the rain nor the sun
to approach them.

Those unspoken words sank
into the soil
entering the roots of trees.
The unceasing wind drew
them upwards in waves
radiating them along branches
from leaf to leaf
and beyond.

There are no ghosts
above that grave.
Nor gods.
There is no memorial stone.

Encased in the cruel grip of time,
a single patti flower
grows upon his grave,
burning bright like a lamp
on a darkened street.

In his final words
lives
the life of our land.

The Memorial

A response to Cheran's 'Grave Song'

She sits in a square in Seoul, wordless
hands clenched, staring steadfastly
at the Japanese embassy.

Deeply rooted as a gingko tree
she is whom the Japanese had called
female ammunition
units of war supplies
public toilets.
She is immovable in snow, wind or sun
cradling a thousand wounds
a thousand tears, a thousand scars.

A bird on her shoulder connects those
who gaze on her to those who have escaped
to the sky. If she could speak, her voice
would be an unending scream, carried
by the wind past street corners, tenement
blocks, paddy fields and pine forests.

Behind her gaze the shadows of those
who have grown old in silence
lengthen in the sun.

Things Happen

When they pepper neighbourhoods with imported
mortars and expansive tank fire. When they
go from house to house lining up girls, women
and men in revenge or on a whim—

When they shut down substations and impose
curfews and travel embargoes so that
market sellers face ruin. When people go
unfed, unwashed and scavenge for scraps—

When they shoot blindfolded men in the back
and take souvenirs of mutilated lives
and hopes. When they rape girls and grandmothers
and celebrate the hecatomb of their success—

things happen
and the world moves on.

Now that the War is Over

During the war they had bagged the bodies
in carpet, sarongs or paddy sacks
and dumped them into the ocean
or by the roadside. Blood seeped into
the earth and the sea and from Manaar
and Manipay, Point Pedro and Kilinochchi
new warriors poured forth, stained by the blood
of those whose call had been answered.

Now, scrambling over the mounds of the fallen,
the carpet baggers are moving in
building hotels and beach resorts
by crimson seas, on crimson sands.
Now, our fishing boats lie encrusted
on the shoreline, the paddy fields are slowly
silting up, our coconut groves are enclosed
by southern hands on northern land.

Now, around Manaar and Manipay,
Point Pedro and Kilinochchi
ghosts retreat into flattened tombstones.
And a barren, dispossessed people
turn eyes that can weep no more
away from the soil and the sea,
to listen to the march of new boots—
now that the war is over.

Blue Lotus Flowers[4]

I
What She Says

Why do you ask me
when he will come?

> He is like the man from the tall hills
> his face hidden by rainclouds.
> The blue of his sapphires glint only
> in the darkness.
> And he comes and goes at will
> like a waterfall crashing down the mountainside.

My tears fall like petals
and wet the plains at his feet.

---

4   This poem has been written in the style of early classical Tamil poetry as laid out in the *Tolkaappiyam*. The poem mirrors the *akam* poems of the classical Sangam period (second century CE) which deal with the interior landscapes of lovers and married life. *Akam* poems use flora and fauna to describe the moods of the narrator – the interior mirrors the exterior and the reader is able to place the path of a relationship based on the landscapes the poems invoke.

II
What She Says

I look to the blue hills
and wait for his return.

> His beauty, like the blooms
> of the tiger claw tree,
> is bright and scarlet in the darkness.
> He is gone, like a heron once fed
> flies to another sky.

My tears run like waves
on a salty shore.

III
What She Says

As the morning dew
wet the green plains
he came to me.

        As beautiful as a peacock on the hillside.
        As strong as a bull elephant
        swaying among the young grass.
        Bright as a green parrot
        skimming the mango tree
        he called to me.

My honey rose and flowed.
The bees made soft music
as he drank his fill.

IV
What She Says

In the forest where the
sparrow hen pecks at the cassia roots
he watched like a stag
warned of a stranger's approach.

>He was strong and wide like a river.
>The plowman harvested by his shore
>and Indran rained flowers
>strewing the ground like a bridal bower.

That was then.
Now I wait for him
trembling for his touch
and my tears water the laurel tree.

V
What She Says

The sun has parched my tears
my bangles slip from my wrist.
Their shards cut my feet
dotting the floor
like the dried kungumum
on my brow line.

> For he has gone to the wasteland
> like a lone hen-eagle searching
> from the branches of the portia tree.
> The mid-day sun burns his feet
> as he stalks, a petulant tiger
> denied its kill.

And here, by my waterless well
bandits threaten my laurel tree.
I have nothing to offer them.
A lizard skittles over the cactus
of my heart.

VI
What She Says

Here by the side of the royal pool
I wait, but he does not come.
He is like the man from the cold shore
scuttling like a crab
to another's bower.

> The cool waters invite me.
> There are no herons
> feeding at my feet.
> The bull elephant has defiled
> the watering hole.

The blue lotus flower opens
its starry petals
offering a pillow for my head.
The waters rise
washing the salt from my eyes.

Village

It is a village, not a camp, somewhere,
beyond the edge of our dreams
where only women live. Survivors
of the various wounds man inflicts
in the name of duty, love or honour.
Here they bloom in palm-leaf huts
and meet under the tree of truth
to nurture their freedom.
A fence of thorns and barbed wire
keeps the world outside. No man
is allowed entry into this space.

Neither is the bougainvillea
with its huge curved thorns which suffocate
as it grows, crushing, drawing blood
revelling in its terrifying will.
With food for their children and jasmine
in their hair the women have no use
for its gaudy swagger.

Instead, their lives progress, as all lives should,
beneath the warmth of a setting sun.

I was Na'amah

I was known by many names and now by none.

I was Na'amah, the pleasant one
mother to all creation. The hourglass
gathered pace in my shadow.

I was Emzara, Betenos, Barthenon
wheat and millet swayed to my song.
Around my feet grew common reed
papyrus sedge and bullrushes.

I was Haykel in Arabic.
Through my mouth sun rose flowers, blue pimpernel
and yachnuk spoke a language of their own.
Cumin and chamomile formed my veil.

In Georgian I was T'ajar, a temple.
Bitter herbs formed my seat.
Out of my left arm grew olive trees,
cypress and cedar of Lebanon. Red bush,
date palms and myrrh out of my right.

I was Nemzar in Armenian.
I knew every lacewing of every petal
every wrinkled bark, each sharp thorn.
I twirled every leaf in dewdrops
and hid a covenant into each rotund kernel.

I was Emzara, Noyemza. Norea to the Gnostics.
The Babylonians called me Tytea.

I was the sunrise of creation
the moon glow of eternity.
In the *Book of Jasher* I was Na'amah
the pleasant one.
Now I am known only as the wife of Noah.

எனது பாடல்கள்
வினோதினி

எனது பாடல்களை நான்
எழுதி முடிப்பது இன்றல்ல நாளையுமல்ல
எனில் என்று?
எழுதாத எனது பாடல்கள்
எல்லாம் அந்தச் சிறுமியின் கைகளில்,
எப்போது வேண்டுமெனிலும் தரமாட்டாளாம்.
தான் விளையாடாதபோது
எடுத்துக்கொள்ளென்கிறாள்.
அவள் தூங்கும்போது முயல்கையில்
ஒரு சொல் வருவதற்குள்
விழித்துக்கொண்டு அவள் சண்டையிட
தோற்றுப்போய்ப் பதுங்கி விடுகிறதென் ஆன்மா
எனது பாடல்களை நான்
எழுதி முடிப்பது இன்றல்ல நாளையுமல்ல
யாருமறியாமல் அவை பத்திரமாக இருக்கின்றன
அந்தச் சிறுமியிடம்

My Songs

by Vinothini

When will I finish writing my songs?
Today? Tomorrow?
Some other day?
Those unwritten songs rest
in the hands of that little girl
who won't release them, easily.
Take them when I am not playing
with them, she says.
Every ambush I set
even as she sleeps
fails – for she wakes
with a fight, tenaciously.
I will not finish writing my songs
today or tomorrow.
Unknown to you,
they are perfectly safe
in the hands of that little girl.

Psalm

A response to Vinothini's 'My Songs'

The name of every MP who voted against the Dubs Amendment (2016), has been used to create both the word 'NO' and the border above it.

Bellingham Clifton-Brown Carmichael Duncan-Smith Wilson Wragg Holobone Malthouse Duddridge Fernandes Allan Baker Stevenson Costa Watkinson Lefroy Green Morris Cleverly Donelan Dowden Elwood Graham Gyimah Parish Scully Selous Tracey Heaton-Jones Kawczynski Norman Carswell Baldwin Barwell Borwick Cartlidge Knight Jenrick Lumley Thomas Tolhurst Warman Jenkin Stewart Hammond Argar Miller Ghani Williamson Howell Leslie Djanogly Morris Gillan Beresford Nokes Rutley Mackintosh Huddleston Stephenson McPartland Elphicke Grant Dunne Grieve Harper Dining Ansell Churchill Davies Mills Coffey Jones Clarke Burrowes

McCartney
Drax   Burt
Freer   Gale
Gove Patel Prisk
Rudd Tyrie Hart
Lord Main Mann
Bingham Tugendhat
Bone Bebb Berry
Offord Nuttall Murray
Penning Newton Johnson
Kinahan Williams Lopresti
R o s i n d e l l Heaton-Harris
Jayawardena Sunak
T r e v e l y a n
Walker Morton
Villiers Stuart
Smith   Smith
Swire   Amess
L e w i s
L i d i n g t o n
Clark   Pow
Whittingdale

Shannon Cash
Ellis   Field
Gibb   Glen
Quin   Raab
Hunt   Hurd
Blunt   Berry
Fox Lee Mak
Smith   White
Pawsey Barclay
M o r d a n t
P a t e r s o n
Wood
Johnson Letwin
Syms Wheeler Pickles
Shapps Fallon Soubry
Stride Evans Evans
Hall May Burns Chalk
Lilley   Fabricant
Prentis   Wright
Liddell-Grainger
R e e s - M o g g
Philip Soames

P e n r o s e
Sturdy Stewart Spelman
Leadsom Robinson Metcalfe
Solloway Murrison Whittaker
L o u g h t o n   P r i t c h a r d
H o l l o w a y   P u r s g l o v e
M e r m a n   S a n d b a c h
S p e n c e r   R o b e r t s o n
W h a t e l y   W o l l a s t o n
M e n z i e s   O p p e r m a n
S w a y n e   S k i d m o r e
M i l l i n g   R e d w o o d
M o r g a n   T i m p s o n
H e r b e r t   Jackson Vickers
Streeter Walker   J o h n s o n
Turner Stewart   W i g g i n
Poulter Lewis   Jenkyns Brazier
B o t t o m l e y   H a n d s
T o m l i n s o n   McLoughlin
Grayling   Crabb   Lancaster
Mowat Gummer Vaizey
Tredinnick   Javid

30

Evennett Freeman Griffiths Goodwill Hancock Bradley Afriyie Aldous Benyon Andrew Chishti
Harrington Haselhurst Henderson Sharma Knight Brokenshire Doyle-Price Drummond Mackinlay
Adams Green Bacon Hinds Pincher Vara Heald Kirby Brady Frazer Gauke Atkins Baron Halfon
Burns Fallon Elliott Campbell Heaped Davies Foster Hopkins Caulfield Davies Maynard Throup
Collins Colvile Double Ellison Garner Sherbrooke Buckland Latham Jones Charting Leigh Garnier
Kennedy Jones Bruce Howlett Morris Chope Harris Milton Simpson Tomlinson Davies Howarth

they said

as
mobilised
children endure
alone on Europe's
dung heaps. They have
hung up their toys their
drums and their harps. They
have nothing left to sing
in this new land.

Meanwhile faith, hope and charity
lie chained and debased
on Albion's shore.

The Last Mango Tree

The last mango tree stands alone
in a garden that was once full
of other mango trees and coconut
palms. It holds out its arms, golden
with fruit, and looks at the rusted, shut gate.
Grass grows beneath and around it
and the birds have grown accustomed
to its solitude. The last mango tree
waits, remembering those years when children
clung to its branches, women picked its fruit –
green for pickling, honeyed orange for eating.
The last mango tree knows that its branches
hold the secrets of a lost people.
It stands guarding memories, surrounded
by abandoned and derelict life.

Gardeners' Question Time, followed by the News

Here they watch each pod for blemishes
compare notes, consult manuals, nip, wrap,
water and fertilise like honey-bees
busily. Here each smug bud blossoms
into a promise ensured and butterflies
lose themselves in sunshine and shadow.

There promises do not bloom but are broken.
There they sow tears and water sorrow.
There the plough catches on things that should not
have been planted, and an anxious people
await a pointless harvest. There, as the sun
hides its face in shadows, even the grass
will not grow and the birds were the first to go.

My Grandfather's House

There is moss growing in the bedrooms
of my grandfather's house.
Green and sticky, staining the walls
and the floor with shades of the sea.
They climb, tracing intricate patterns, around
browned squares, where pictures used to hang.

The roof has fallen in. Water stagnates
on a cushioned floor as disturbed bats circle,
drawing the night in. The rooms are empty
of all that was him. The doors have been locked
warped and unwilling to open onto
a tomorrow which does not contain him.

It is six o'clock and the mosquitos
gather noisily in rooms that once
smelt of sweet margossa leaves.
They are the music makers, the sum total
of our dreams. The inheritors of rooms
that reek and sweat in angry dismay.

There is moss growing in the bedrooms
of my grandfather's house and raindrops
sing a lament on deserted floors.

Acknowledgements

With thanks to the editors of the following magazines and anthologies, in which versions of some of these poems were first published: *Modern Poetry in Translation*, *The North*, *London Grip New Poetry*, *Nivedini: Journal of Gender Studies* (Sri Lanka), *Silenced Shadows* (Amnesty International). My thanks also to Ilkley Literature Festival and to Geoff Brokate of *The Cohere Project* for commissioning some of the poems appearing here.

My heartfelt thanks to the generosity and counsel of Jack Mapanje, who read my early work and encouraged me to re-engage with my mother tongue. To Lakshmi Holmström who was a kind yet exacting mentor, whose coattails I will always follow. To Sasha Dugdale for her friendship and support and to the *Modern Poetry in Translation* family, who gave my work its first home. To Cheran and Vinothini for allowing me to translate their work; to the many talented Tamil poets from Sri Lanka, whose work is an inspiration to me.

My heartfelt thanks to Peter and Ann Sansom for their support and faith in my work. To Peter for helping me sculpt and shape these poems and from whom I have learnt so much. To Katie McLean from The Poetry Business for her help and expertise, and for persevering with errant Tamil fonts. To Anna Honing who read early drafts of some of these poems. To Sasha Dugdale and Vidyan Ravinthiran for their advice on the manuscript. To the many poets writing in the UK whose work has nurtured and inspired me.

My heartfelt thanks to my friends from Sri Lanka, spread out across the world and to my friends in York who accompanied me on each step of this pamphlet.

Finally, my heartfelt love to my husband Richard and to my children, Kit and Becky, who have made this borrowed land my home.